Happy Birthday

_____

with love,

_____

date

_____

Stories, sayings, and scriptures to Encourage and Inspire

hugs™

for your Birthday

STEPHANIE HOWARD

Personalized Scriptures by
LEANN WEISS

HOWARD
PUBLISHING CO.

To my kid sisters,
Pamela Dianne
and
Angela Michelle

Our purpose at Howard Publishing is to:

- *Increase faith* in the hearts of growing Christians
- *Inspire holiness* in the lives of believers
- *Instill hope* in the hearts of struggling people everywhere

Because He's coming again!

Hugs for Your Birthday © 2004 by Stephanie Howard
All rights reserved. Printed in the United States of America
Published by Howard Publishing Co., Inc.
3117 North 7th Street, West Monroe, LA 71291-2227

04 05 06 07 08 09 10 11 12 13   10 9 8 7 6 5 4 3 2 1

Paraphrased scriptures © 2004 LeAnn Weiss, 3006 Brandywine Dr.
Orlando, FL 32806; 407-898-4410

Edited by Between the Lines
Interior design by Stephanie D. Walker

Library of Congress Cataloging-in-Publication Data

Lynne, Stephanie, 1974–
   Hugs for your birthday : stories, sayings, and scriptures to encourage and inspire/
Stephanie Howard ; personalized scriptures by LeAnn Weiss.
      p. cm.
   ISBN: 1-58229-349-X
      1. Birthdays—Religious aspects—Christianity. I. Weiss, LeAnn. II. Title.

   BV4597.555.L96 2004
   242—dc22

                                                      2003057121

Contents

your Birthday

A Day to Reminisce

CHAPTER
1

Remember the days of old and reflect on past generations. **Meditate** on all **My works** and consider the **great** things I've done. Think about everything that's **true** and **noble.** Remember whatever is **right,** pure, and lovely. **Focus** on whatever is **admirable,** excellent, or **praiseworthy!**

THINKING OF YOU,

Your Rock of Ages

—from Deuteronomy 32:7;
Psalm 143:5; Philippians 4:8

Remember when…

Just saying the phrase stirs up feelings of warmth and happiness. There's something about rec-ollecting the past that feels good. All five senses seem to partake in the memories.

Recall your father working in the yard, and you can still hear his distinctive hum. Reminisce about a grandmother's homemade bread, and you can almost smell the familiar, yeasty scent. Remembering a childhood bike accident conjures up the painful feeling of a broken arm. The bitter taste of unsweetened lemonade lingers when you recall your early attempts at entrepreneurship. Close your eyes, and you can still see the weathered lines on your grandfather's face, even though he's been gone for many years.

Yes, something in our very

being needs to reminisce. We each have a particular yearning to bring back moments in time when life seemed simpler. Your life is an amazing collection of experiences and events that have made you the individual you are. The good times brought you joy and laughter. The difficult times encouraged strength and character.

What are some of your favorite recollections? What are some of your not-so-favorite memories? It might be that your best memory is of a time when someone remembered you.

Whether the experience is sweet or bittersweet, it's good to remember the people and places that have shaped you. Time passes quickly. Before you know it, this birthday will also be a fading memory. Take a moment to reminisce about the past.

The memory is a wonderful treasure chest for those who know how to pack it.

BARBARA JOHNSON

A Gift from the Past

"Grandma, I'm home!" Josh called out as he entered the charming three-bedroom cottage. Hanging his car keys on the nail beside the door, he walked directly to the kitchen where he found his seventy-eight-year-old grandmother baking.

"Josh! You're home early. Hungry?" Eloise Foster placed a plate of warm sugar cookies on the kitchen table, then sat down next to her nineteen-year-old grandson.

Josh nodded, choosing the largest cookie. "My professor let us out early after we completed the

exam. I think I did pretty well." He put the entire cookie in his mouth and selected another.

"Good." Eloise smiled and rose from the table. "I was just getting ready to take some goodies to the retirement home." She pointed to the remaining cookies. "These are for you."

"Thanks, Grandma. I'll save the rest for later." Josh pushed his chair away from the table and then kissed his grandmother on the cheek. "I've got to study."

Eloise smiled as she watched him walk out of the kitchen. It was a privilege to have her grandson living with her while he attended college away from home. When she first heard that Josh was looking for inexpensive housing, Eloise offered her spare bedroom and bathroom freely. She had doubted he would accept—young men rarely choose to live with their grandmothers. But with few options and little money, Josh had jumped at the opportunity.

Having Josh around was motivation for Eloise to stay active. She loved giving her time to help others. Having her grandson around to be the recipient of her efforts made it that much sweeter. Since her husband's death three years ago, she had struggled to keep herself busy. With no one left to take care of, she had searched desperately for new responsibilities to fill the void. Baking was one of her favorite pastimes and a natural diversion. Now most of her days were spent baking breads and cookies for those whose activities were more restricted—friends and strangers alike. But she was pleased that Josh's presence filled the remaining empty spaces in her life.

When she returned from delivering her goods, Eloise found Josh at the table eating a supper of leftovers from the night before. He pointed to a black-and-white photograph lying on the counter. "Hi, Grandma. I found this in my closet—is that you and Granddad?"

Eloise looked at the picture and chuckled. "Oh my, that was a long time ago. I must have overlooked it when I was cleaning to make room for your things."

The young couple in the picture held each other cheek to cheek, beaming proudly. Although at first glance the elderly woman hardly resembled the teenage girl in the photograph, a closer look revealed

A Gift from the Past

that perhaps time hadn't changed her all that much. The beautiful smile and dancing eyes were the same. And many of the girl's favorite pastimes were still enjoyed by the woman even at this stage of her life. "Yes, that's your granddad and me before we were married. We met at a school dance. I loved to dance, and he was a good dancer." Eloise smiled, enjoying the memories that came flooding back. "After we married, we rarely had time to go dancing. But every once in a while, after the children went to bed, we'd pull out the record player and dance in the backyard under the stars."

Leaning back in his chair, Josh appeared to be enjoying the story. "Wow, Granddad was quite a romantic guy!"

"He was very romantic. Even after fifty-three years of marriage, he never stopped demonstrating his love in unique ways. If there were more men in this world like your granddad, there'd be fewer marriages falling apart."

Josh contemplated a moment. "I have a feeling he'd say the same thing about you. That's a long time to be married."

"Yes," Eloise agreed, "but not long enough. I still miss him dearly." She shook her head, attempting to scatter the lonely thoughts that were beginning to form. "Well, I'm sure you've got better things to do than sit around talking about the good old days."

"Well," Josh said, straightening his chair, "I do have a lot of work to do. But I've enjoyed hearing about you and Granddad. And I needed a break."

"Don't stay up too late," Eloise advised, tousling Josh's hair. "You'll be worthless tomorrow."

"I have a feeling I'll be pulling an all-nighter," Josh informed her.

Eloise shook her head sympathetically. "If that's the case, I'll leave out plenty of sustenance before I retire."

Knowing that refusal of her offer wasn't an option, Josh thanked his grandmother with a hug. "I don't know what I'd do without you, Grandma."

"You'd be nothing but skin and bones!" she answered with a wink.

The next morning Eloise was already mixing ingredients for a pound cake when Josh groggily emerged from his bedroom, backpack slung over

A Gift from the Past

one shoulder. "Good morning!" Eloise sang out to greet him.

"Good morning." Josh smiled sleepily and rubbed his eyes. "I talked to Mom on the phone last night. Why didn't you tell me today's your birthday?"

Eloise dismissed the question. "Now, why would I? There's no reason to bring that up. It's a day like any other day."

That answer wasn't good enough for Josh. "At least I could take you out for dinner or something."

"Nonsense, Josh. You're strapped for cash as it is. Spending time reminiscing with you last night was the perfect birthday present," Eloise stated firmly.

Josh stuffed an orange in his sweatshirt pocket and peeled a banana. "Well, I'm giving you a present whether you like it or not. You've done too much for me to let this day pass without doing something special for you."

"Please, just save your money for textbooks. I don't need a thing!" Eloise argued.

"Have a good day, Grandma," Josh hugged her, ignoring her plea.

Eloise went about her day as usual, visiting friends, all the while hoping Josh wouldn't try to find a gift for her. She really had everything she needed, and having him around was the sweetest gift she could ask for. *Besides,* she thought, *after seventy-nine years, if I don't have everything I want, there's no use trying to get it now.*

When she arrived home later that evening, Josh met her at the door. "Wait just a minute, please," he said, holding up a finger as he backed away from the door.

Eloise realized he had disregarded her previous request. "Josh, I told you—" She stopped midsentence as soft music started playing nearby.

Returning to the door, Josh took his grand-mother's hand and led her through the house to the backyard. Eloise gasped quietly when she saw what he'd done. Paper lanterns glowed against the dusky sky, tracing a circle across the lawn. A small TV tray held Josh's CD player and a vase of handpicked flowers. The melody drifted gently through the trees.

A Gift from the Past

Josh grinned guiltily, "It's the best I could do with such short notice."

Eloise was speechless, knowing how much effort had gone into Josh's surprise. She wasn't sure if she was moved more by the picturesque setting or the fact that her stories of the past had made such an impression on him.

"Happy Birthday, Grandma." With pride, Josh held out his hand. "Would you care to dance?"

With bleary eyes, Eloise swallowed to clear the lump in her throat. "I'd love to, Josh." *Maybe,* she thought, *there are still a few gifts to look forward to after all.*

your Birthday

A Day to Treasure Family

CHAPTER

2

I've given you **great treasure** in ordinary earthen vessels so you'll be able to see My **power** and **glory** within and not be distracted by what's on the outside. I've made My light **shine** on you to **brighten** your heart with the knowledge of My glory as revealed in the **face of My Son.** When you face loneliness, struggles, and hardships, don't fear being crushed or destroyed. Remember, your **heart** will be where your treasure is. **Heavenly treasures** are eternal: They can't be stolen or destroyed.

TREASURING YOU,

Your Heavenly Father

—from 2 Corinthians 4:6–9;
Matthew 6:20–21

eternal

heavenly

You've heard it said: "You don't know what you've got until it's gone." That holds true especially with those we love. Sometimes life can become so hectic that we forget to really communicate with our families. Sure, we talk and interact about daily necessities; but meaningful, thought-provoking dialogue is often neglected.

When was the last time you stayed up until the wee hours of the morning because you just couldn't stop talking to someone you loved? A simple question about future plans could inspire hours of heart-to-heart conversation. Sometimes it's during those midnight talks that family grows more precious and you come to the realization that you are truly loved.

And you *are* truly loved. Whether those around you have taken the time to say it or not, you're admired. Your family may say it in the little things. Like saving that last piece of pie for you because it's your favorite. Or listening to that same old story again because they know you love to tell it.

Today, find opportunities to spend intimate, one-on-one time with each member of your family. Don't wait until you have a large block of time to share. Steal moments from each day to connect with others. Take a break from routines and enjoy special occasions with those you love. Laugh and make memories. Appreciate the people, heritage, and traditions that make up your family. It may just be the best gift you can give yourself.

Home is not where you live but where they understand you.

CHRISTIAN MORGENSTERN

Far from Home

Lance Corporal Christopher Davis sat on the steps outside his barracks holding his head in his hands. His camouflage uniform was filthy and soaked with sweat. He clunked the heel of his combat boot on the ground to dislodge several layers of mud. His stomach growled loudly, although he barely felt the hunger pains, having grown accustomed to the sensation.

Christopher had spent the last four months stationed in Cuba, but for the past three weeks he'd been "in the field." With no showers, little food, and

not much opportunity for sleep, the field was designed to train soldiers to live in warlike conditions. Right now Christopher was so exhausted, he felt like he'd been through a real battle.

Slowly he pulled himself up and trudged to the room he shared with Bobby, a fellow marine. Emerging from the bathroom, Bobby shook water from his hair. "It's all yours," he said, tucking his towel securely around his waist. "There's no hot water though."

Struggling to pull off a clinging, smelly sock, Christopher shrugged. "Cold water sounds good right now. I've had just about enough of this tropical humidity."

Bobby nodded in agreement. "Yeah, taking a shower hasn't stopped the sweat from dripping down my back. But at least I don't stink!"

"I guess that's all we can ask for in this weather," Christopher answered with a tired laugh as he headed for the bathroom.

As cool water sprayed, dissolving the grime from his face, Christopher tried not to think about how he was going to be without his family for a whole year. When he had gotten the orders to go to Cuba for twelve months, he dreaded telling his wife and two young sons that they wouldn't be able to accompany him. They'd done their best not to complain too much, but he knew it would be just as hard on them as it was for him. Not only did he miss them terribly, but Christopher also felt guilty about leaving his wife to raise their children alone for such an extended time.

Standing in front of the sink, he examined the beard that had grown in since his last shower almost a month ago. "Well, I might as well shave before my birthday dinner." He knew tonight's meal in the chow hall would be no different than the regular rotation of meat loaf or macaroni and chili. But at least it sounded better than their meals in the field. He'd had his fill of vacuum-packed meals sufficient in calories but less than satisfactory in flavor.

Worn jeans and a white T-shirt felt weightless after weeks of carrying his military gear. Grabbing the small stack of letters that had connected him to home over the past months, Christopher left the room and went to get something to eat.

Far from Home

The mess hall was nearly empty, with only ten minutes left before closing. Rather grateful for the solitude, Christopher carried his tray to an empty corner table. He was glad to find orange gelatin for dessert instead of his least favorite, green gelatin with marshmallows. Bowing his head, Christopher silently blessed his food.

Although he was grateful for many things besides the meal, Christopher couldn't help feeling that this was one of the worst birthdays ever. Taking a large bite of meat loaf and mashed potatoes, he picked up one of the envelopes he'd brought from his room. It was the most recent letter from his family.

Distance and time apart had made Christopher treasure his family more than ever, and reviewing the old letters seemed to bring them a little closer. Still, reading about their activities was bittersweet. Christopher couldn't help but laugh thinking about his seven-year-old son, Michael, losing a tooth in the middle of Sunday school. He hated that he'd missed five-year-old Thomas's first T-ball game. Even though his sweet wife, Susan, insisted that they were making it "just fine," he knew it had to be hard disciplining the boys without help and dealing with her own loneliness.

Christopher folded the letter and scooped up a few more bites of the meat loaf, saving the orange gelatin for last. Picking up one of the more tattered papers, Christopher saw the picture Michael had drawn. Although it was supposed to be cheerful, Christopher felt depressed. Stick figures of his wife and children stood in front of their house, while his representation was beside a faraway tree—a painful reminder that the separation was as hard on his family as it was on him.

Christopher barely tasted his dessert. He headed back to his room feeling guilty for not being around for Susan and the boys, and more lonely than ever. Bobby was just leaving the barracks. "Hey, Chris, you have some mail in the room, and there's a package too."

"Thanks." With a glimmer of hope, Christopher quickened his pace. He could only suppose that the package was from his family.

Rounding the corner, Christopher immediately noticed the large box on his bed. *I don't even want to*

Far from Home

think about how much it cost to mail a package that size. The thought flashed through his mind but was gone in an instant, replaced by his excitement. Sure enough, the label bore Susan's familiar handwriting.

Christopher pulled out his pocket knife and slit the packing tape carefully, so as not to damage any of the items inside. Near the top of the box, under a thin layer of wadded up newspaper, was a large, manila envelope.

Anticipation was at its peak as he tore open the envelope to find a small stack of photographs. He laughed out loud when he saw the images. The first was a picture of his two children wearing birthday hats and standing in front of a birthday cake. Suddenly a small detail caught his eye, and Christopher held the photo closer, not sure he believed what he saw. But it was true. On the cake, in bright red icing letters, were the words "Happy Birthday, Dad!" The second picture showed the boys blowing out candles on the cake.

The third photo quickly became a blur through his tears. It was considerably crooked, obviously taken by one of the boys. As Christopher roughly wiped his cheeks with the back of his hand, Susan looked back at him, smiling as she held a piece of cake out in front of her as if offering it to him. The last snapshot showed the boys each enjoying a rather large piece of his birthday cake. Christopher laughed affectionately, squeezing more tears out of his smiling eyes.

He put the pictures aside and curiously explored the rest of the parcel. Although there was no birthday cake to be found, he was delighted to find a large plastic bag stuffed with his favorite dessert, Rice Krispies Treats. Without a moment's hesitation, he chose the largest he could find and bit down greedily. Christopher closed his eyes to savor the moment. It tasted just like home.

Next he unpacked a dried-macaroni necklace from Thomas and a folded piece of newsprint, most likely a new drawing from Michael. Christopher felt a catch in his heart and held his breath as he started slowly unfolding the paper. What message would he see in this innocent work of art? *Don't read too much into it*, he told himself as he opened the final fold.

With one glance, Christopher heaved a sigh and

Far from Home

grinned broadly, even as his eyes welled up again with tears. There was only one way to interpret this masterpiece, as far as he was concerned. Across the top of the page was written in childlike cursive, "What I want to be when I grow up." Below was a stick figure of Michael, outfitted in what only a trained parental eye would recognize as his brown and green camouflage uniform. It was all the indication Christopher needed to be assured that he was still an important part of his family and could have a positive impact on his children.

With pride, Christopher held the picture to his chest. Even though he was far from home, his family was close at heart. This wasn't the worst birthday after all.

your Birthday

A Day to Start Over

CHAPTER
3

Because of My great **love** for you, I will not allow you to burn out or be consumed. My **compassions** and **mercies** for you are new every day. Watch Me do a **new** thing! I will **make a way** in the desert and **provide streams** in the wasteland of your life. Be confident that I'll **complete** the good work I've begun in **you.**

GRACIOUSLY,

Your God of New Beginnings

—from Lamentations 3:22–23; Isaiah 43:19; Philippians 1:6

Birthdays are all about new beginnings. You probably were more aware of that concept as a child. Kids can hardly wait for their next birthday to come around. In fact, time seems to pass ever so slowly for youngsters anticipating their big day. They announce their age proudly, adding "and a-half" or "and three-quarters," depending on how much time remains before they can claim another year. Children know that with a new age come new gifts, new experiences…a new life.

Maybe you're in need of a new life. Perhaps you aren't satisfied with the path you've been taking. It's not too late to change your course. Don't allow past mistakes to dictate your future. Today is the perfect day to start over.

The apostle Paul provides encouragement for those in need of a new beginning: "Put off your old self;…be made new in the attitude of your minds; and…put on the new self, created to be like God in true righteousness and holiness" (Ephesians 4:22–24).

Or maybe you can think of a relationship that would benefit from a fresh start. It's never too late to forgive and allow broken hearts to mend.

Today can be the beginning of a new chapter in your life. You can experience a rebirth every year by simply letting go of bad habits and negative self-talk. Whatever it is that holds you back from a rich and rewarding life, let it go. Make this the birthday you start over and live the life you desire.

Live life to the fullest by learning to forgive and forget.

MARY C. CROWLEY

A Birthday to Share

I should have known nothing would change! Shawna fumed as she cleaned up the remains of their picnic supper. It had been three years since she'd seen her younger sister, Mattie, and within the first few hours of their reunion they were already arguing. Shawna gathered the dirty containers and headed toward the house, sorely tempted to slam the door as a message to Mattie, still in the backyard. *No,* she decided, *someone's got to act like an adult; it might as well be me.*

Shawna looked out the window over her kitchen sink as she cleaned the dishes. *If only I could enjoy*

my sister as much as my kids do, she thought wistfully as she observed her two children playing a game of tag with their aunt. *After all, it's my birthday too.*

Shawna and Mattie had been born on the same day two years apart and always shared a strong sibling rivalry. Combined birthday parties were the norm because it was cost-effective for their parents, but the girls hated having their birthdays on the same day. Looking back, it seemed a year didn't go by without an argument flaring up for one reason or another. Shawna and Mattie always found it necessary to debate who they thought had received the best gifts or who had more friends at the party.

It was sadly predictable, then, that this birthday was beginning to resemble all the ones from their childhood.

Shawna dried her hands and threaded the towel through the cabinet door handle. Procrastinating her expected return to the festivities, she decided to clean up the living room instead. *Let the kids spend some quality time with their aunt,* she rationalized.

But with each toy she retrieved from the floor, Shawna began to feel a little sorrier for herself.

Falling into the old, familiar pattern, she began comparing her life with her sister's. *She has it so easy—no major commitments like a husband or kids to take care of. Even her job isn't normal. A freelance graphic designer. Her whole life is arranged so she's free to do whatever she wants, without having to consider anyone else.*

Shawna tried to stifle her rising feelings of jealousy. But as a divorced mother of two, she couldn't help but think of how nice it would be to spend just one day in her sister's shoes. "She doesn't know how good she has it," Shawna grumbled aloud, then took a deep, weary breath and braced herself to rejoin her sister and children in the backyard.

"Mom, come play with us!" the kids called to her.

Shawna shook her head but managed to feign cheerfulness. "Nah, I'll just watch."

"C'mon, 'Mom'!" Mattie chided.

Before Shawna could make up a reasonable excuse, Andrew, her seven-year-old son, yelled, "Tickle Torture!" commanding his aunt and younger sister, Ally, to join his attack on their mother.

The children tickled Shawna relentlessly while

A Birthday to Share

Mattie held her down, ignoring her cries for release. At last they all collapsed on the lawn, exhausted and breathless from laughter.

"OK, kids," Shawna finally said as she pulled herself reluctantly off the cool grass. "It's almost dark—time for your baths."

The children moaned in protest. "Do we have to?" Ally pleaded, hugging Mattie tightly around the waist. "We're having fun with Aunt Mattie!"

"Sorry," Shawna answered kindly but firmly. "You both have school tomorrow. You have to get up too early in the morning to stay up past your bedtime tonight."

Andrew adopted his best sad face. "Can't we play just a little bit longer?" It was the look and tone that most tore at Shawna's heart, and for a moment she wavered, looking at her watch. But she knew how grumpy he and Ally would be in the morning if they didn't get enough rest.

"Not tonight," she said, apologetically shaking her head. "By the time your baths are finished, it will already be more than an hour past your bedtime."

Then Mattie piped in. "Shawna, a little less sleep isn't going to kill them. It's only this one time."

Shawna's ears started to burn as she tried to restrain her returning irritation with her sister. It was difficult enough to hold the line with her children without having her take their side. "Excuse me, but I'll thank you kindly to leave the parenting to the *parent!*"

Mattie responded defensively. "I'm not trying to interfere, but—"

"But you *are*," Shawna interrupted hotly.

Shawna turned toward the children who stood silently beside her and announced with final determination, "It's time for your baths."

This time without hesitation, Andrew and Ally walked directly toward the house. Shawna and Mattie followed in silence.

As she supervised the bathing and tucked Andrew and Ally into bed, kissing their foreheads and looking at their sleepy and satisfied faces, Shawna's anger subsided. She knew in her heart that Mattie hadn't meant to cause trouble. She only wanted to spend some time with the only family she

A Birthday to Share

had. Shawna turned off the lights and went downstairs to try to smooth things over with her sister.

She found Mattie on the porch, staring into the darkness. Shawna quietly and tentatively sat down next to her, building up the courage to apologize. But Mattie spoke first.

"Sorry about what happened earlier."

Shawna shrugged and swallowed hard, saddened that their birthday had again devolved into painful tension. "I guess old habits are hard to break."

Both sisters still stared straight ahead until Mattie again broke the silence. "Do you remember the time in high school when we brought our report cards home and you had straight A's, and I had straight B's? Mom and Dad were so proud of you that we went out for pizza that night. They didn't stop talking about it for weeks. It was like they wanted to make sure I knew how much smarter and more responsible you were than me."

"No, it was never like that!" Shawna replied defensively. "They just chose to highlight different achievements for each of us."

Mattie chuckled sarcastically. "Yeah, I guess you just had a lot more achievements…"

Shawna simply closed her eyes, too tired for another argument. *Here we go again.*

"Shawna, I've never told you this, but I'm very proud of you," Mattie said quietly.

Stunned, Shawna looked at her sister. The sentiment was so unexpected that it seemed to take all the air from her lungs, and she didn't know how to respond.

Mattie took Shawna's hand as she continued. "You're a great mom. You show such patience and love with Andrew and Ally. Your children are yet another of your many admirable achievements. They're lucky to have you as their mom." Mattie's lip quivered with her final admission. "And I'm lucky to have you as a sister."

In the blur of emotions at Mattie's words, tears had begun to flow down Shawna's cheeks. Suddenly she realized she had waited a lifetime to hear those words of love and admiration from her sister. Now the wall of pride and bitterness dissolved so easily that Shawna regretted it not happening sooner.

A Birthday to Share

Reaching out to each other, the two sisters hugged and sobbed. "We've wasted too many years fighting," Shawna cried. "I'm so sorry I've held on to my grudges. I'm so sorry we've been sisters but not friends."

Mattie pulled away to look Shawna in the eye. At last, after years of guarded competition, the rivalry over childish things was gone. "Let's start over, right now."

Shawna nodded fiercely. "Yes. No more judging, no more jealousy."

Mattie squeezed her arms in agreement. "From now on, let's try to support each other and understand each other better."

Shawna's eyes glistened in agreement to their new pact. The two sisters sat arm in arm, quietly watching the stars twinkle above. As Mattie leaned her head against her sister's shoulder, Shawna savored the new feelings of warmth and peace taking root in her family.

"Happy birthday, big sister," Mattie whispered.

Shawna smiled as she kissed the top of Mattie's head. "Happy birthday to you, little sis."

your Birthday

A Day to Celebrate

CHAPTER
4

Even before you were born, I **planned** all of your days. Don't settle for merely surviving. I came to give you **abundant life.** I know the **plans** I have for you. My plans will **prosper** you and not harm you. **Watch** Me fill you with all **joy** and **peace** as you **trust in Me.**

CELEBRATING YOU,
Your Creator

joy

peace

—from Psalm 139:16; John 10:10; Jeremiah 29:11; Romans 15:13

The older we get, it seems, the less fanfare we seek on our birthdays. Unless we're marking a new decade, we tend to ignore the day's significance and treat it like any other. That's an unfortunate mistake.

We had the right idea as children. We need to relearn some of the necessary elements of a birthday: having friends over for cake and ice cream; laughing a lot, even playing silly games; taking pictures or recording the event on video. In other words, allowing others to celebrate with us.

Don't pass up the balloons and streamers on the pretext of their being too much trouble. After all, your birthday only comes around once a year. Bask in the love your family and friends shower on you. Enjoy being the center of attention for a few moments. As grownups, that doesn't happen often enough.

Hopefully this isn't a day you meet with anxiety or dread. Your birthday should evoke feelings of excitement and anticipation. Don't waste time fretting about getting older—you've got too many things to experience and appreciate.

Even the Scriptures tell us to celebrate: "This is the day the LORD has made; let us rejoice and be glad in it" (Psalm 118:24). Not only has God offered you the gift of life, but He also has given you family and friends to share it.

On your birthday, celebrate your blessings! Celebrate the miracles in life that tend to get overlooked. You're alive! This is a wonderful day!

Let someone else run the world for a while. Jesus took time for a party...shouldn't we?

MAX LUCADO

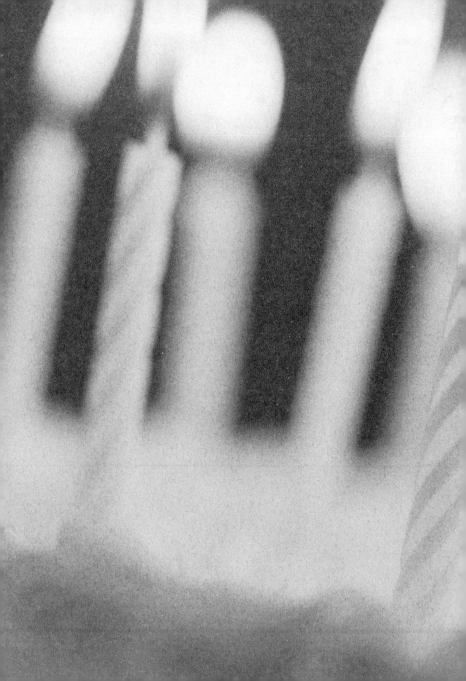

Racing Time

Marcie tapped the small squares on the calendar, counting down to the one circled in bright red ink, then shook her head in disappointment. "I'm not ready," she murmured. In less than three weeks, not only did she plan to "celebrate" her thirty-fifth birthday, but she also hoped to run a five-mile race. Of course, that was a goal she had set six months ago, when she was full of the enthusiasm that prompted her New Year's resolutions.

At the end of last year, Marcie had been over-weight, single, and depressed about both. She

decided then that getting her life in order would be the best birthday present she could give herself. So she had hired a personal trainer to help her work out three days a week, consulted a dietician to help her revamp her meals, and gotten involved in several ministries at church to meet new people.

Now, taking a new urgency from the calendar, Marcie stretched her hamstrings one last time and jogged out the door. "I knew I was setting my goals too high," she called out to Joyce, her trainer, as the two women met on the sidewalk. "There's no way I'll be ready to run five miles by the end of this month!"

"Sure you will!" Joyce replied in her usual assuring, energetic voice. "I have every confidence that you can finish that race." She patted Marcie on the shoulder as they began a slow jog. "It wasn't long ago that you could barely run for two minutes. Now you run two miles without stopping!"

Marcie nodded, but she still wasn't convinced. "I guess we'll just have to wait and see."

"Like I always say, 'One step at a time.'"

As the women rounded the third block of the neighborhood in concentrated silence, Marcie reminded herself that she'd come a long way since her first workout session with Joyce. Upon their initial consultation, walking swiftly for more than ten minutes had left Marcie panting. They had worked up to sixty minutes of fast-paced walking before they tried running. Now, not only could she run two miles, but she was fifty pounds lighter. *Even if I don't run the whole five miles, I'm proud of my accomplishments. Now all I have to do is find a husband...*

"Great workout, Marcie!" Joyce said when they finished the run.

Still breathing hard, Marcie placed her hands on her hips and began her routine of squats and lunges. "Yeah, I feel pretty good today."

"Good," Joyce said, smirking and taunting good-naturedly. "Next time we'll kick it up a notch and see what you're really made of."

Marcie rolled her eyes and laughed. "That's the last time I ever tell *you* when I'm feeling good!"

As she made her way home, Marcie ran through her mental list of chores for the rest of the weekend. *Laundry, shop for new running shoes, buy groceries... boring! Not much to celebrate for a thirty-fifth birthday.*

Racing Time

She was happy with the way her lifestyle had improved, but it was difficult not to think about her love life—or rather, her lack of one.

She turned the key and entered her apartment, the cool relief of air conditioning washing over her. A deep sigh escaped her, a mix of satisfaction and sadness, and she headed for the shower. She surveyed her flushed cheeks in the bathroom mirror. Beads of perspiration still clung to her forehead. "I'm not desperate—just picky," she confirmed to her reflection as she pulled the rubber band from her tousled, brown hair.

Marcie could have dated more than she did. Invitations from men still came frequently enough. But she had decided that at this point in her life, she didn't want to invest time and energy in a relationship with someone she didn't consider marriage material. "Why bother dating Mr. Wrong and allow Mr. Right to pass you by?" she explained to those who didn't understand her reasons for remaining unattached. It just seemed that Mr. Right was taking his own sweet time to come her way.

After stocking her refrigerator with some groceries from the corner market, Marcie spent the rest of the afternoon shopping for shoes. With all the brands and styles to choose from, she wanted to take her time finding the perfect fit. She still clung to the hope that the right running shoe would somehow keep her feet from feeling the torture she would be putting them through. *And if not, at least I'll look good at the race*, she thought with a smile.

The sporting goods store's display wall was loaded with at least a hundred styles of women's athletic shoes, and Marcie wasn't even halfway through examining the running shoe section when a male voice interrupted her perusal. "Marcie, is that you?"

She turned but didn't recognize the voice or the tall, handsome man holding a stack of three shoeboxes. "Yes, it's me." Marcie smiled, but her mind was racing through a catalog of old acquaintances to find a match before her forgetfulness became obvious.

"I'm Derek. We were in the same business management class in college. I know it's been a while."

He smiled warmly, and Marcie breathed a sigh of relief at being rescued.

"Oh yes, I remember." Secretly Marcie was flattered. Of course she remembered Derek—who wouldn't remember someone so smart and good-looking! "I'm surprised you recognized me—I've changed a bit since then."

"Well, you look great!" Derek quickly but not quite imperceptibly scanned her toned physique before changing the subject. "Is there anything I can help you with?"

"Oh, do you work here?" Marcie was a little embarrassed to suddenly notice his store-embroidered nametag, but it didn't escape her that Derek's left hand lacked a wedding band.

"Actually, I'm the owner. I started out as manager after graduation, and a couple of years ago I bought out the previous owners." Derek smiled again, and his hazel eyes seemed to sparkle as he gazed into Marcie's. "So I pretty much live here."

Marcie felt her usual reservation melting away. *I'm enjoying this a little too much.* She stifled a giggle and forced her attention back to her goal. "I need some new running shoes. I'll be running in a race downtown later this month."

"Let me show you a few different pairs." Derek offered. "I do a lot of running myself and can tell you which designs are the lightest and give the best support."

Thirty minutes later, Marcie was the proud owner of a pair of stylish yet comfortable running shoes. She handed Derek her debit card and thanked him. "Maybe these shoes will help me finish all five miles. I need all the help I can get!"

"I'm sure you'll do great," Derek said with enthusiasm as he handed her a pen to sign her receipt. "I'd offer to run with you, but I'll already be at the finish line. I always set up a booth at local races to promote the store."

"That's very kind of you," Marcie replied, instantly embarrassed that her comment wasn't quite right. *Ugh! That sounds like I meant placing the booth was kind, which is silly—I meant he was kind to offer to run with me!* Flustered, Marcie hurried to exit. "Well, I guess I'll see you at the finish line."

Racing Time

"Sure! I'll even save you one of our free T-shirts," Derek promised, waving as she left the store.

Marcie tried not to feel giddy about her brief encounter. *After all,* she told herself, *I have no idea if he's available. Maybe he's always that nice to his customers.* Unless she suddenly had a need for new sport socks, she'd just have to wait until the race to see him again.

At the next training appointment, Joyce was surprised at the level of improvement in Marcie's performance. "Where did that extra burst of energy come from? Something tells me it isn't just the new shoes!"

Marcie smiled as she breathed heavily. "They are great shoes, but I have an even better incentive."

"Really?" Joyce asked with interest.

"I met a really nice guy the other day, and he'll be waiting for me when I finish the race." Marcie enjoyed the surprise on her friend's face and the look of eager anticipation as she told of her meeting with Derek.

Joyce laughed, approving of the assurance she had seen grow in Marcie over the last few months.

"Wow, Marcie, what if he's 'the one'?" Joyce said, half teasing, half dreaming for her friend.

Marcie couldn't deny that the thought had entered her mind, but she refused to nurture it. There were still too many unanswered questions. But suddenly she felt eager for the race—and to truly celebrate her thirty-fifth birthday. Sporting a grin that hinted at her new excitement and optimism, Marcie shrugged with calm confidence. "Maybe so. But like you always say…"

The two women recited their motto in unison: "One step at a time!"

Racing Time

your *Birthday*

A Day to Look Forward

CHAPTER
5

My **joy** is your **strength!** I continually guide you and **satisfy** your **desires** with **good** things. I've given you **birth** into **living hope** and an eternal **inheritance.**

LOVING YOU,
Your Everlasting Father

—from Nehemiah 8:10; Isaiah 58:11; 1 Peter 1:3–4

When was the last time you blew out your birthday candles and actually made a wish? If you're like some people, your main objective is extinguishing the flames before someone calls the fire department. Or maybe you hurry through the ritual because you feel pressured by onlookers eagerly waiting for a piece of cake. Perhaps you just haven't given much thought to what you would wish for.

Yet birthdays are the perfect opportunity to think about what you want for your life—to make goals for years to come. Wouldn't it be great if each year you could honestly say that you had accomplished all you set out to do?

Take a moment today to consider what you're doing to positively affect your future. Set some goals: What

do you want to accomplish in the years ahead?
Create a realistic strategy for making those hopes
and dreams a reality. Visualize where you'd like to be
in five, ten, and twenty years—and start working now
toward that end.

Remember, your heavenly Father has made special
plans for your future. "'I know the plans I have for
you,' declares the LORD, 'plans to prosper you and not
to harm you, plans to give you hope and a future'"
(Jeremiah 29:11). So next time you hear that
familiar birthday tune and friends and family
are gathered to watch you to blow out your
candles, take a moment and look to the
future. Don't just take a deep breath
and blow. Close your eyes and
make a wish!

I believe that God has a dream for each of us, and our greatest challenge and joy lies in finding and following that dream wherever it may lead.

HEATHER WHITESTONE

Promise

Jenna stared at her reflection in the mirror. Having spent the last thirty minutes arranging her hair, she still couldn't decide on a style. She had attempted everything from a French twist to a French braid, but nothing seemed suitable for her big date. She was going for a specific look. After all, this was her sixteenth birthday. She wanted to appear mature without trying too hard.

Glancing at the dress on her bed, she smiled. Her mother had taken her on a special shopping trip just for this day. The midnight blue gown had rhinestone

spaghetti straps, and the hem fell just below her knees. Not only did it flatter her figure, but it also was the perfect complement to her dark blue eyes. From the moment she first saw it, Jenna knew the dress would be hers. Her mother knew it too, because Jenna couldn't stop gliding in front of the dressing room mirror to see it from different angles.

Looking back in the mirror at her long blond tresses cascading freely over her shoulders, Jenna sighed. *Well, I guess simple is always elegant.* She ran the bristles of a large brush through her hair one last time, then slipped into her new dress and shoes.

A soft knock on the door told her it was nearly time to go. "Come in," Jenna sang, bubbling with nervous excitement. She knew it would be her mom coming to examine her complete ensemble.

Jenna's mother gasped when she saw her. "Jenna! You look stunning!"

"Thank you." She twirled confidently upon her mother's admiration. "I hope Daddy thinks so too."

"Of course he will," her mom insisted with a proud glow. "He's waiting downstairs for you right now."

With a final glance in the mirror, Jenna turned toward her mother. "OK, I'm ready."

Descending the stairs to the living room, Jenna saw her father waiting. He too was dressed in his best suit and smelled faintly of aftershave, and he smiled his approval. "You look beautiful, Jenna."

Suddenly the poise she exuded in front of her mother was replaced with the self-conscious timidity of an adolescent. "Thank you, Daddy. You look handsome too."

Ever since Jenna could remember, her father had taken her on special "dates." Whether celebrating an achievement or simply sharing an ice cream cone and discussing current events, Jenna had always loved their one-on-one time. And going on dates like her parents and other adults made her feel special.

But tonight's date was met with even greater anticipation because never before had it been such a formal affair.

Jenna's mom joined them and held up her camera. "Let me take some pictures. It's not every day that our baby girl turns sixteen."

After they had exhausted what seemed like every possible pose, it was time to go. Mother and daughter hugged tightly, then the two adults exchanged a knowing glance. "You two have a wonderful evening," Jenna's mom said, ushering them out the door.

"We will," Jenna's dad said with a wink.

Jenna blew her mother a kiss, then took her father's hand as they walked to the car. She could hardly contain her excitement during the drive downtown. She had never been to Palmo's, the upscale Mediterranean restaurant even her parents only visited on the most special occasions. Palmo's required reservations a month in advance, and local celebrities were frequently spotted there. Jenna hoped she would appear as sophisticated as this occasion made her feel.

A hostess greeted them in the softly lit foyer, and Jenna stayed close to her father as they waited for their table. As they were escorted to a small booth, she tried to look around without gawking, hoping to see some familiar faces. She didn't recognize anyone, but she nudged her dad when she saw a man who looked like he could be "someone." Her father chuckled at her excitement about rubbing elbows with the rich and famous.

After Jenna and her dad had ordered their entrées, she relaxed a bit and took in her surroundings. The candlelit tables and unique sound of Greek music were far from characteristic of her simple, teenage life, and she felt privileged to be "let in" to this adult world of experience.

"Daddy, I'm having a wonderful time! Thank you for bringing me here," Jenna said, flushed with delight.

"I'm glad you're enjoying yourself." He reached into his pocket. "I have something for you."

Jenna couldn't imagine this evening being any more special, and she certainly hadn't anticipated a gift. Her joy and anticipation grew as her dad pulled out a small, black velvet box.

"Your mother and I have been planning this evening for a long time. As a matter of fact, we've been praying for this day since you were a little girl."

Flattered and curious, Jenna waited for her dad to continue. What could be so special?

Promise

"As parents, we've always encouraged you to be a young woman of virtue and character. As a father, I want to inspire you to live a life of purity as well. Now that you're sixteen, you're allowed to go on dates with other boys, not just your dad." He offered the box to Jenna. Slowly and carefully, she opened it and looked inside.

"Oh, Daddy!" She gasped with surprise and delight. Jenna lifted the beautiful ring from its case. A delicately crafted gold heart encircled a diamond that, though small, sparkled magnificently under the candlelight.

Jenna looked at her dad just in time to catch the emotion in his eyes. "This diamond," he explained reverently, "represents your purity. The heart represents the love you will share with your husband alone. I would like you to wear this ring, signifying your promise to save yourself for marriage."

Jenna's mind was whirling. She felt honored at the respect and affection her dad obviously held for her, and she was moved to learn that her parents had been praying for her and thinking of her dating and marriage even before she had been interested in boys.

She closed her eyes and imagined the kind of relationship she wanted to have with her future husband. She knew one thing for sure—she wanted to feel like this—like a treasure.

Slowly and resolutely, Jenna placed the symbolic gift on her left ring finger. "I'll wear it until I have an engagement ring someday." She slid out of the booth, walked around to her father's side of the table, and wrapped her arms around him in a tight hug. She kissed him on the cheek and whispered, "This is the best birthday ever! I'm so lucky to have you as my dad!"

Throughout the evening, Jenna couldn't stop admiring her ring. She chatted animatedly, waving her hand as she talked so she could watch it glitter. When she picked up her water glass, she adjusted her finger so the light was refracted in her diamond.

Adding to an already perfect evening, the maître d' surprised Jenna with her own personal birthday cake. As she took a breath to blow out the solitary candle,

Promise

she glanced up to see that its soft radiance only further illuminated the look of love and pride on her father's face.

With a dramatic puff, she blew out the candle. She was certain that if she found someone to love and cherish her as much as her father did, all of her wishes would indeed come true.

your Birthday

A Day to Receive

CHAPTER
6

E very **good** and **perfect** gift in your life is a **blessing** from Me. I **love** to do far **beyond** all that you can ask or **dream** by My power working in you. Surely My **goodness** and **love** will **surround** you every day of your life!

ABUNDANT BLESSINGS,

Your God of Wonder

—from James 1:17; Ephesians 3:20; Psalm 23:6

Everybody loves a surprise. Even if you're one of those people who say you don't like surprises… deep down inside, you really do.

Yes, it's nice to know beforehand what to expect from life, but that's seldom possible. And would you really want to know everything in advance, even if you could?

Surprises are fun. Unexpected gifts are sometimes the best kind to receive. Doesn't it feel good to find out that someone cared enough to want to honor you? Just think about how much effort and planning it took to keep you unaware of the scheme! When people give, it shows that they love. Whether the gesture is simple or grand, the message is the same. They went out of their way because you've had an impact on their life.

Perhaps you're more comfortable with giving than receiving. A generous attitude is commendable. But some treasures in life can't be gained by one's own effort. They can only be received as a gift.

Forgiveness is one such amazing gift. It cannot be purchased or bargained for. It is given freely as the ultimate gesture of love. God offers forgiveness to everyone who believes in Him.

Can you recall other "gifts" God has sent your way? A sunny day when the forecast predicted rain. An unexpected friend in your moment of crisis. A bonus when finances were tight.

On your birthday, consider all the special gifts you've received and express thanks to those who gave for sharing their love.

Life is a gift
that God has given us.
MOTHER TERESA

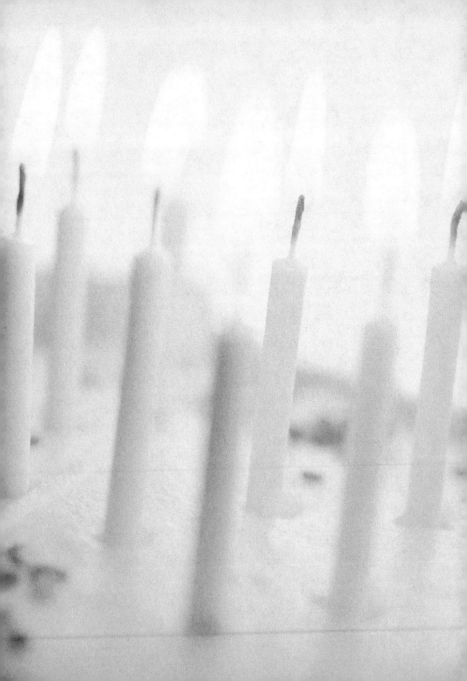

A Bid for Love

The convention room was decorated beautifully. Brenda was proud of how well she had transformed the large, drab space into a warm, inviting area for the auction. The proceeds would benefit Jeannie, a family friend who was struggling with her second bout of breast cancer. Party planning was Brenda's specialty, so she didn't hesitate when asked to coordinate the event.

She scanned the room, noting with satisfaction that several volunteers were busy preparing their stations. A minimum of two hundred guests were

expected, and Brenda was going over her mental checklist to be sure everything was ready. She strolled over to inspect the refreshment corner. Trays of crackers and cookies lined one table; a large punch bowl and rows of clear plastic cups were spread out on another. Nodding in approval, Brenda turned toward the platform where Sandra was organizing items to be sold.

"Sandra! I can't believe how many things came in to be auctioned. You did a great job getting people to donate," Brenda said with admiration. "I've never been good at asking people for donations."

"It was easy," Sandra replied. "When people hear about the cause, their hearts just swell with compassion. Nearly everyone I asked gave something."

"I know Jeannie is grateful for all that's been done for her. I hope this is a success." Brenda looked at her watch. "OK, everyone," she announced over the activity and chatter. "It's almost time to open the doors."

Sandra walked hurriedly down the long row of tables to ensure that everything was in place.

Brenda turned to take her post at the punch bowl, but as she did, something on the auction table caught her attention. Surrounded by an assortment of antiques was a small figurine of a woman and daughter. Brenda couldn't believe her eyes. It was the one piece she lacked from her collection.

She began collecting the mother-and-daughter figurines nearly thirty years earlier, after giving birth to her own daughter, Cheryl. Then, Brenda had collected them simply because of their intricate beauty. She couldn't have known the inexpensive porcelain would become so valuable after the series was retired. Unfortunately, she only possessed five and had never come across the sixth and final piece.

Brenda walked toward the table and picked up the coveted piece. Rotating it for closer inspection, Brenda was struck by how lovingly the daughter rested her head on the mother's shoulder as they embraced. The timeless pose perfectly depicted the relationship Brenda and her daughter had always shared.

Much to Brenda's surprise, the porcelain was flawless. Not a chip or blemish could be found, even

A Bid for love

though the piece was at least twenty-five years old. She held her breath as she turned over the price card and let out an astonished gasp. Though the original piece hadn't been more than ten dollars, today's bidding would begin at one hundred!

Still, Brenda couldn't bear the thought of passing up this sought-after treasure. *I might have to splurge just this once,* she thought as she carefully set the piece back on the table. *I can make it an early birthday present for myself.*

As guests streamed in, Brenda worked steadily, filling punch glasses. It was a larger crowd than even she had hoped for, and she'd barely even been able to greet people she knew as they passed by. But one familiar voice caught her attention.

"Hi, Mom!"

Brenda looked up to see Cheryl reaching for a drink.

"Cheryl! Can you believe this turnout? We've sold more than three hundred tickets so far!" Brenda exclaimed as she added more punch to the large serving bowl.

"I know—it's wonderful!" Cheryl agreed. "Someone even donated a fishing boat and a car! I hope this will help with some of Jeannie's medical bills."

"Me too, sweetie. She needs all the help she can get."

"I'm going to sit down. The auction will begin soon." Cheryl waved as she walked away.

With so many guests to attend to, Brenda didn't have time to participate in the auction. She did, however, keep her eye on the mother-and-daughter figure and hoped it would somehow escape the notice of other bidders.

The crowd thinned as the auction wound down, and Brenda took the opportunity to pick up a numbered paddle so she would be able to bid from her post at the table.

Shortly after, the beautiful porcelain sculpture was up for bid. With number 182 in hand, Brenda made the first entry.

To her dismay, two consecutive bidders quickly raised the price to two hundred dollars. Brenda raised her paddle to offer two hundred and fifty dollars.

A Bid for love

For a moment, she thought that she had won. Then paddle 135 shot up from the middle of the crowd, bidding three hundred dollars.

"Do I have three-fifty?" the auctioneer called, looking at Brenda at the back of the room.

Brenda clenched her jaw. She hated to spend that much money on something that would only sit and collect dust. Even though the piece had sentimental value, she wondered if it was really worth all this.

Her heart won out. *All right, one last effort*, she decided. She waved her paddle.

"Let me hear four hundred!" The auctioneer solicited loudly.

Brenda stood still, searching the crowd for movement and hoping she had prevailed. Her heart sank when paddle 135 popped up once more.

This time when the auctioneer called for Brenda to bid four hundred and fifty dollars, she shook her head and forced a smile, trying to hide her deep disappointment.

"Going once, going twice...sold!" The auctioneer pointed to paddle 135.

Brenda swallowed the lump in her throat, clapped politely, and turned back to the punch table. *It's just a statue*, she tried to console herself. *It would have been ridiculous for me to spend that much money on it.*

As the event came to a close, Brenda busied herself cleaning up. She was proud to learn that more than $11,000 had been raised for Jeannie. As she was bidding farewell to the last departing guests, Brenda felt a tap on her shoulder. She turned to see Cheryl waiting with her purchases from the day.

"Here, Mom," she said, handing her a paper bag. "I know your birthday isn't until next month, but I can't wait!"

Brenda held the bag without opening it. "What's this?"

"Just open it!" Cheryl said excitedly.

Placing her hand inside the bag, Brenda knew with one touch what the package held. The surprise and emotion registered unmistakably on her face as, slowly, she lifted from its wrapping the beautiful sculpture of mother and daughter embracing.

"It was you! You had paddle 135!" Brenda cried.

A Bid for Love

With a look of confusion, Cheryl answered, "Why...yes. When I saw the sculpture, I knew it was the one piece you never found for your collection. But I almost didn't get it. There was another bidder in the back of the room—"

Suddenly Cheryl understood. "Were you the other bidder?"

Brenda nodded with exasperation. "If I had known, I wouldn't have kept bidding! Cheryl, you shouldn't have bought this. You spent far too much!"

Cheryl shook her head with determination. "Mom, you never let me buy you anything. Besides, there may not be another opportunity to complete your collection. The money went to Jeannie, anyway. I don't regret it one bit."

Brenda looked down at her beautiful prize. Her daughter's gesture of love made it that much more valuable, and she couldn't stop her eyes from misting with emotion. "Thank you, Cheryl. I love it." Still holding tightly to the figurine, she extended her arms to her daughter.

"Happy Birthday, Mom." Cheryl stepped toward her mother.

With eyes closed, and with an uncanny resemblance to the porcelain figurine, Brenda and Cheryl held each other in a sweet embrace only a mother and daughter could share.

your Birthday

A Day to Discover Self

CHAPTER
7

O utwardly, you aren't getting any younger. Your physical strength and beauty will decline with time. But **inwardly**, I'm **renewing** you day by day. Your present troubles won't last **forever** but will yield a **great reward** someday. When you wait and **hope** in Me, I'll **renew** your **strength.** I'll help you live life without growing weary or giving up.

RENEWING YOU,

Your Everlasting God

—from 2 Corinthians 4:16–17; Isaiah 40:31

forever

everlasting

Look at yourself. No, don't go find a mirror—but you may want to get a pen and paper. Spend a few moments reflecting on who you are. Take inventory of things you've done that you're proud of. Include what you have yet to accomplish or become. Think about mistakes you've made and what you've learned from them.

Don't let our culture fool you. Who you are cannot be defined by your age or by any other material standard. Sure, the world would like to convince you that having a youthful physique and a smooth, unblemished face are some of the factors that determine your worth. In reality, though, the beauty of your disposition and mindset are more important. Peter, one of Jesus' disciples, wrote: "Your beauty should not come from outward adornment…. Instead, it should be that of your inner self, the unfading beauty of a gentle and quiet spirit, which is of great worth in God's sight" (1 Peter 3:3–4).

Do you bring out the good in others? Does your name come to mind when people think of someone compassionate and generous? Do you build up the people around you, encouraging them to pursue their aspirations? The answers to these questions will help you understand who you are.

Even if you find that you're lacking in some of these areas, you'll be inspired as you make some positive adjustments in your life. In the process, you may discover just how much there is to love about yourself.

Love is not a matter of counting the years—it's making the years count.

WOLFMAN JACK SMITH

A New Reflection

The high-scale, trendy salon buzzed with the usual activity of a Saturday morning. Sitting under the hair dryer, Paula hastily flipped through a fashion magazine. Her annoyance grew with each page she turned. Having set eyes on too many advertisements of youthful, half-starved supermodels, Paula wished she'd chosen a *Reader's Digest* instead.

Peering around the room didn't help either. It was filled with hairdressers and their clients who appeared to be half her age.

Why did I come here? she wondered, increasingly

aware that a new hairstyle wasn't going to make her feel any younger.

Paula hadn't revealed to her stylist that it was her forty-eighth birthday. She'd simply asked for a new color and a fresh-looking haircut. Her other little secret was her desire to be transformed into the woman she was twenty years ago.

The past several months had brought a series of changes in Paula's life. Since her youngest daughter left home for college, Paula had struggled to find her new identity. She no longer felt useful as a stay-at-home mom, yet she hadn't found another place to fit in. She considered joining the work force, but there weren't many openings for someone whose experience was limited to parenting. Her husband, Jack, had encouraged her to go back to school and finish the degree she'd been working toward when they started their family. The idea was exciting—and intimidating. Truth be told, Paula feared her own future. She dreaded feeling old...looking old.

Turning her attention back to her magazine, she frowned at the page. The article portrayed a beautiful actress in her midforties. Reading through the list of this talented woman's accomplishments made Paula feel even more inadequate.

Finally her hair style was complete, and Paula examined her reflection in the mirror. The color looked good, but her attention was riveted on the wrinkles around her eyes and mouth. *Ugh! If only I had the money...* Paula could think of several areas she would love to have a plastic surgeon correct.

She quickly paid for her haircut and left the salon. Feeling even more disheartened than she had before her new look, Paula walked to her car with purpose. She was desperate and determined to find something that would make her feel significant and exciting.

"Maybe I'll look into skydiving," Paula muttered sarcastically as she drove home. "Rock climbing might be fun..." But suddenly the idea of trying something daring and dangerous was appealing. Paula liked the fact that she didn't know anyone her age who had dared to try either of those activities.

Paula passed by a trendy plaza and spotted one of her daughter's favorite clothing shops. She made a U-turn. *A stylish outfit might be what I need,* she reasoned.

A New Reflection

But before she had turned off the ignition, a group of girls emerged from the store with bags in hand, chatting animatedly. Seeing their young bodies clad in fitted, revealing clothes was a reality check. Paula knew that wasn't the look she was going for. She'd feel ridiculous parading in the same clothes her teenage daughter would wear. Shoving the car in reverse, she backed out and headed home.

Feeling defeated, Paula entered the quiet house. She didn't know why Jack wasn't home yet, and it aggravated her depressed condition. They were supposed to go out to celebrate her birthday. Defending against the notion that she'd been forgotten, she went to her closet to select a semiformal dress for the evening.

The phone rang, and Paula hoped it was her husband with some explanation for his absence. "Hello?"

"Hi, sweetie," Jack said. "I know I'm a little late for our date, but I'll be home in a few minutes. I hope you'll be ready to go when I get there. I have a surprise for you."

Paula felt a little better knowing that Jack hadn't backed out on their date or forgotten her birthday.

As she was touching up her makeup, Paula heard the sound of a noisy muffler growing closer—and louder—outside her window. Slightly annoyed, she went to look outside and was shocked to see her husband driving a large motorcycle up their driveway. "What on earth?!" She wondered if perhaps Jack was experiencing his own midlife crisis.

Paula opened the front door just as Jack hopped off the orange Honda with red flames painted along the sides. Taking off a matching helmet, he grinned.

"What is this?!" Paula asked incredulously. "It had better not be my birthday present."

Jack chuckled and shook his head. "No, I borrowed it from a friend for our date tonight." Noting her slender dress and heels, he added, "You may want to change your clothes though."

Paula hadn't seen Jack on a motorcycle since their courtship nearly twenty-seven years earlier. And though it hinted at the pleasant memories of those long-ago days, this wasn't exactly how she had

A New Reflection

planned to spend her birthday. She wanted to protest, but since Jack seemed excited, she turned around silently and went inside to change.

This time Paula emerged wearing flatteringly snug but comfortable khaki pants and a knit sweater. Jack revved the engine as he handed her a helmet. "Here, put this on."

Paula hated to smash down the youthful hairdo that had taken all morning to achieve. With great reluctance, she put on the helmet and mounted the bike. She wrapped her arms around Jack's waist and yelled over the roar of the engine. "Where are we going?"

Revving the accelerator, Jack sped down the driveway. "Wait and see," he called over his shoulder.

Paula found herself actually enjoying the ride across town. She still hadn't figured out where Jack was taking her, but the tension she had felt earlier in the day was dissolving. The warmth from his back felt good as the crisp evening air blew past them. She closed her eyes and abandoned the uncertainties that had been consuming her.

By the time Jack came to a stop, Paula felt invigorated. She opened her eyes to find that they had come to the state park where Jack had proposed to her. Jack grasped her hand and led her down a romantic, pebbled path. As they strolled, they reminisced about their courtship and all the fun times they'd had at this park. Paula could hardly believe how quickly time had passed.

As the trail curved around some trees, Paula suddenly saw what Jack had prepared for her. In the same meadow where she had accepted his hand in marriage, a large picnic basket was set on an old quilt by a stream—very similar to the way it had been all those years ago.

Jack motioned for her to sit down on the blanket and then sat beside her. "I've noticed that lately you've been feeling down about getting older. I see how you look in the mirror and frown at what you see."

Gazing intently and lovingly into her eyes, Jack continued. "But tonight, I want you to see things differently—to remember what I felt for you when we were dating…and what I still feel for you. Our lives have changed a lot over the years, but in our hearts, we're still the same. No…we're better. I love you for the amazing, beautiful woman you've become." He kissed her hand tenderly, then put his arm around her shoulder. "No matter how you feel right now about getting older, I want you to know that as far as I'm concerned, you've still got 'it.' And I will always want it."

A lump had risen to Paula's throat during her husband's sweet declaration of love. She was ashamed that he had noticed what now seemed like a silly struggle, and she vowed that from that moment on she would take realistic steps to redefine her life.

Her new goal felt far more appealing than the feeble attempts to look twenty years younger. In fact, she realized with a start, she suddenly was *feeling* younger.

Leaning close to Jack, Paula wrapped her arm around his waist and looked into his eyes with deep affection. "Thank you, honey."

As they relaxed in each other's embrace, Paula's peaceful smile spread into a girlish grin. "I sure had fun riding that motorcycle. Wouldn't it be fun to have one of our own?"

Jack raised his eyebrows, and the corners of his lips curled in impish delight. "We can definitely look into it."

Paula giggled softly. With her head on his shoulder, she noticed her reflection in the water. She saw a middle-aged, less-than-perfect mother and wife…and smiled.

Look for these other *Hugs*™ books:

HOWARD
PUBLISHING CO.